Ohio

by the Capstone Press
Geography Department

Reading Consultant:

Harvey Alston

CAPSTONE PRESS

MANKATO, MINNESOTA

C A P S T O N E   P R E S S

818 North Willow Street • Mankato, MN 56001

Printed in the United States of America.

Library of Congress Cataloging-in-Publication Data
    Ohio/by the Captone Press Geography Department
    p. cm.--(One nation)
    Includes bibliographical references and index.
    Summary: Gives an overview of the state of Ohio, including its history, geography, people, and living conditions.
    ISBN 1-56065-439-2
    1. Ohio--Juvenile literature. [1. Ohio.]
    I. Capstone Press, Geography Dept. II. Series.
F491.3.038 1996
977.1--dc20

                                    96-23437
                                     CIP
                                      AC

Photo credits
G. Alan Nelson, cover, 10, 15, 32.
Ohio Dept. of Travel and Tourism, 4, 8, 21.
Unicorn/A. Gurmankin, 5 (left); Martha McBride, 5 (right);
    Daniel J. Olson, 16; Russell Grundke, 26.
FPG, 6.
Cheryl Blair, 18, 34.
James Rowan, 22, 25.
Root Resources, 28.
Kay Shaw, 30.

Table of Contents

Words in **boldface** type in the text are defined
in the Glossary in the back of this book.

Fast Facts about Ohio

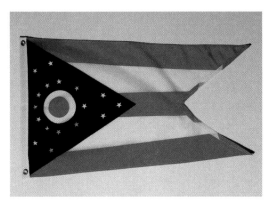

State Flag

Location: In the Great Lakes region of the Midwestern United States
Size: 44,828 square miles (116,553 square kilometers)

Population: 10,847,115 (1990 United States Census Bureau figures)
Capital: Columbus

Cardinal

Scarlet carnation

State bird: Cardinal
State flower: Scarlet
  carnation
State tree: Buckeye
State song: "Beautiful
  Ohio," by Ballard
  MacDonald and Mary
  Earl

**Date admitted to the
  Union**: March 1,
  1803; the 17th state
Largest cities:
  Columbus, Cleveland,
  Cincinnati, Toledo,
  Akron, Dayton,
  Youngstown, Parma,
  Canton, Lorain
Nickname: The
  Buckeye State

Buckeye

Chapter 1
Rock and Roll

In September 1995, a museum opened in Cleveland. This museum has no paintings or dinosaur bones. Instead, it displays guitars, costumes, and music. It is the Rock and Roll Hall of Fame and Museum.

I. M. Pei designed the museum. The building sits on the shore of Lake Erie. Its 162-foot- (49-meter-) tall tower rises from the water. A glass roof covers the building.

Sights and Sounds in Rock's Museum

The museum shows and tells the history of rock music. One floor honors rock's great stars.

Visitors to the Rock and Roll Hall of Fame and Museum can view taped concerts of the Beatles.

The Midwest's only Sea World is in Aurora.

Visitors listen to music from the 1950s through the 1990s. They can watch filmed concerts of the Beatles and Elvis Presley. **Deejays** spin records for live radio broadcasts from the museum.

The museum has more than 4,000 items on display. Jimi Hendrix's handwritten **lyrics** for "Purple Haze" are there. So is John Lennon's Sgt. Pepper uniform.

Picking Cleveland

In 1951, deejay Alan Freed first used the words "rock 'n' roll." This happened during a radio broadcast from Cleveland. In 1952, Cleveland hosted the first rock concert. That is why Cleveland was picked to have the museum.

About 60,000 people visit rock's museum every month. Shoppers and office workers crowd the streets near the museum.

Rolling in the Buckeye State

Ohio also has some great amusement parks. Sandusky's Cedar Point has 11 huge roller coasters. The Demon Drop is 13 stories high. King's Island is near Cincinnati. Its Beast is the world's longest roller coaster.

Ohio also has water fun. Cincinnati's Coney Island has watercoasters and bumper boats. Aurora has the Midwest's only Sea World.

Chapter 2
The Land

Ohio lies in the far eastern part of the Midwest. It is a Great Lakes state. Lake Erie forms most of Ohio's northern border. The lake's shoreline stretches for 312 miles (499 kilometers).

The Ohio River forms the state's southern border. It also forms part of its eastern border. Ohio's lowest point is on the Ohio River. This is sea level.

The Great Lakes Plains

The Great Lakes Plains lie along Lake Erie. This is a narrow strip of flat land. Fruit trees, grapes, and vegetables grow well there.

Fog covers Turkey Creek Lake in southern Ohio.

Michigan
Lake Erie
Pennsylvania
Toledo
Cuyahoga River
Cleveland
Maumee River
Sandusky River
Indiana
Campbell Hill
Muskingum River
Columbus
Cincinnati
Scioto River
Ohio River
West Virginia
Kentucky

Cleveland, Sandusky, and Toledo spread out along the lake. Good ports and rivers make them important shipping centers.

The Maumee River ends at Maumee Bay. That is just north of Toledo. The Sandusky River ends in Sandusky. The Cuyahoga River winds through Cleveland. These rivers empty into Lake Erie.

12

Off the coast are several small islands. Kelleys Island and the Bass islands are the largest ones. State parks and national wildlife **refuges** are on them.

The Till Plains

The Till Plains cover most of western Ohio. **Glaciers** once moved over this land. They left rich soil called till. Today, corn and soybeans grow there.

Columbus, Cincinnati, and Dayton are on the Till Plains. Columbus stands on the Scioto River. The Miami River flows through Dayton. These rivers empty into the Ohio River. Cincinnati sits on the Ohio.

Campbell Hill is the highest point in Ohio. It is northeast of Dayton. This hill rises 1,550 feet (465 meters) above sea level.

Many Till Plains lakes were formed by dams. The largest of these are Grand, Indian, and Delaware lakes.

The Appalachian Plateau

The Appalachian **Plateau** covers most of eastern Ohio. Rolling hills and valleys cross the northern plateau.

Steep hills and valleys mark the southern plateau. Narrow streams rush between the southern hills. Many streams tumble over waterfalls. The Muskingum and Hocking rivers flow through the plateau. Dillon Lake is on the Muskingum River.

Wayne National Forest covers 202,967 acres (81,186 hectares) in the southeast. Large stands of pine and cedar trees grow there.

Rich mineral deposits lie under the plateau, including coal, oil, natural gas, clay, and salt.

Wildlife

Eagles, egrets, and herons live along Lake Erie. Bass, catfish, and perch swim in Ohio's lakes and rivers. Deer, fox, and mink live in its forests.

Lake Erie forms most of Ohio's northern border.

Climate

Ohio's summers are warm and **humid**. Its winters are cold. Strong winter winds sometimes bring blizzards along Lake Erie.

Southwestern Ohio receives the most rain and snow each year. Northwestern Ohio receives the least. Tornadoes cross the state in spring and early summer.

Chapter 3
The People

Ohio is one of the smallest Midwestern states. Its population, however, ranks seventh in the nation. Ohio grew quickly during the 1800s. Since the 1970s, this growth has slowed.

American Settlers

Ohio's first white settlers came from eastern states. Moravian **missionaries** moved from Pennsylvania. They founded villages along the Tuscawaras River.

Farmers left Massachusetts and Connecticut. These easterners wanted Ohio's rich farmland.

Ohioans crowd the streets of Circleville for a pumpkin fest.

The Amish live simple lives. They drive buggies, not cars.

They settled along the Ohio River. Many also founded towns along Lake Erie.

Amish farmers also left Pennsylvania. They settled from Geauga through Ashland counties. Today, the Amish still live simple lives. Their homes have no telephones or electricity. They work their fields with horse-drawn plows. Ohio has the largest number of Amish in the nation.

European Immigrants

In the early 1800s, German, Welsh, and Irish **immigrants** arrived. The Germans settled on farms. Some worked in factories. Welsh miners found jobs in southern Ohio. The Irish helped build Ohio's railroads and **canals**.

From the 1880s through the 1920s, other Europeans arrived. They came from Italy, Poland, Russia, Hungary, and Czechoslovakia. Most of these newcomers worked in Ohio's factories. Today, about 88 percent of Ohioans have European **ancestors**.

African Americans

Almost 11 percent of Ohioans are African Americans. Many African Americans arrived in Ohio in the 1800s. It was a safe place to live. Slavery was never allowed in Ohio.

Many African Americans ran businesses. Others owned farms. Ohio laws, however, kept African Americans separate from whites. They could not attend white schools or churches.

In 1856, Wilberforce University was founded. It was the nation's first university for African Americans.

Many white Ohioans were part of the Underground Railroad. Southern slaves sought freedom across the Ohio River. Ohioans then led the slaves to Canada.

In the early 1900s, many more African Americans moved to Ohio. They came for jobs in Ohio's factories.

Today, Cleveland, Cincinnati, and Columbus have large African-American neighborhoods. The National Afro-American Museum and Cultural Center is in Wilberforce.

Native Americans

By 1842, Ohio's Native Americans were removed from the state. Today, about 20,000 Native Americans again live there.

Ohio's Native Americans do not live on **reservations**. Every year, Native American groups meet near Loudonville. They celebrate with traditional dances, music, and food.

A child plays at Ohio's Sea World.

Other Ethnic Groups

A little more than 1 percent of Ohioans are Hispanics. Most of them emigrated from Mexico, Puerto Rico, and Cuba.

Ohio also has a growing Asian-American population. Columbus has the Midwest's second-largest Chinese population.

Toledo has a large Lebanese community. Many of their ancestors arrived in the early 1900s.

Chapter 4

Ohio History

Mound builders lived in Ohio about 1,000 years ago. Some mounds served as graves. Others were used for special ceremonies.

By the 1600s, Native American groups lived in Ohio. They included the Shawnee, Miami, Wyandot, and Delaware.

The Struggle for Ohio

In the early 1700s, French and English traders crossed Ohio. Both England and France claimed the Ohio Valley. England had 13 **colonies**. They were east of the Appalachian Mountains. Some colonists wanted to move into Ohio.

American troops were stationed at Fort Meigs during the War of 1812. The fort near Perrysburg is a state memorial.

In 1763, France lost its North American lands. England gained all land east of the Mississippi River. This included Ohio.

The Revolutionary War

In 1776, the English colonies declared their independence. They fought England in the Revolutionary War. The colonists defeated English troops in Ohio.

In 1783, the English signed a peace treaty. England recognized the United States of America.

The Northwest Territory

In 1787, Ohio became part of the Northwest Territory. Thousands of settlers moved into Ohio. Cincinnati, Cleveland, Dayton, and Youngstown were founded.

The Indians fought to keep their land. In 1794, they lost the Battle of Fallen Timbers. They gave up most of their land in Ohio.

The State of Ohio

In 1803, Ohio became the 17th state. Columbus became the permanent state capital in 1816.

A canal boat navigates the Miami and Erie Canal.

The United States fought the War of 1812 with England. The United States won the Battle of Lake Erie. This kept the Great Lakes in the United States.

After the war, more settlers poured into Ohio. Many followed the Ohio River. Others took the Erie Canal. It linked New York with Lake Erie.

Ohio built canals. They linked Lake Erie and the Ohio River.

The Civil War

By 1860, the issue of slavery divided the United States. States south of the Ohio River still allowed slavery. The northern states had banned slavery.

In 1860 and 1861, 11 southern states left the Union. The Civil War started in April 1861. About 350,000 Ohioans fought for the Union of the North. In 1863, southern cavalry raided Ohio. Union forces captured them. In 1865, the South **surrendered**.

New Industries

After the war, new companies started in Ohio. Two rubber plants opened in Akron. John D. Rockefeller formed the Standard Oil Company in Cleveland. Other companies made steel, machinery, and furniture.

World Wars and the Great Depression

The United States entered World War I in 1917. Ohio built airplane parts and trucks. The state's rubber and steel also helped win the war in 1918.

Actors re-enact a Civil War battle near Burton.

Ohio is an important steel-producing state.

Good times continued for Ohio's factories in the 1920s. Warren G. Harding became president of the United States in 1921. He was from Marion.

In 1929, the Great Depression hit the nation. Many Ohio factories closed. Nearly half of Ohio's workers lost their jobs. The government started special projects. Workers built dams along Ohio's rivers.

The United States entered World War II in 1941. This helped end the Depression. Ohioans built Jeeps. Others made airplanes, ships, and weapons.

Recent Changes

Ohio stayed busy after the war. Its cities grew. New workers found jobs. The St. Lawrence Seaway opened. It linked Lake Erie's port cities to world trade.

During the 1970s and 1980s, many companies left Ohio. They moved south for cheaper labor and better weather. Thousands of Ohioans lost their jobs. Ohio became part of the Rust Belt. Empty factories in the Midwest turned to rust.

Ohio also had **pollution** problems. Fish were dying in Lake Erie. The Cuyahoga River once caught fire from waste fuels.

By the 1990s, Lake Erie was clean enough for fish. Many Ohio factories now make plastics. Service businesses have become more important.

Chapter 5
Ohio Business

Manufacturing is the single largest part of Ohio's economy. But service industries employ the most people. Banks, insurance companies, and stores are some service businesses. Farming and mining also play important roles in Ohio.

Manufacturing

Motor vehicles and parts lead Ohio's manufactured goods. Automobiles and trucks are made in Lorain, Lordstown, and Toledo. Cleveland, Dayton, and Toledo make car parts. Aircraft parts come from Akron, Cleveland, and Columbus.

Fountain Square is in downtown Cincinnati. Tourism is an important industry in the city and state.

Ohio's farmers raise wheat, corn, soybeans, and potatoes.

Cincinnati has the nation's largest soap factory. Only Indiana makes more steel than Ohio. Rubber tires and glass are other products made in Ohio.

Agriculture

Ohio's farmers raise corn, wheat, soybeans, and potatoes. Tomatoes, sweet corn, and cucumbers grow near Lake Erie. Apples, peaches, strawberries, and grapes grow there, too.

Dairy and beef cattle provide meat and milk. The Poland China hog was bred in the Miami River valley. Ohio's sheep produce the most wool east of the Mississippi River.

Mining

Southeastern Ohio has large coal and natural gas mines. Oil is still mined in eastern and northwestern Ohio.

Ohio also produces sandstone, clay, limestone, and salt. The nation's deepest salt mine is near Fairport Harbor. It is about 2,000 feet (600 meters) deep.

Service Industries

Ohio is headquarters to many national chains. Cincinnati is home to Kroger. The Limited is based in Columbus. Wendy's headquarters is in Dublin.

Shipping is an important Ohio service business. Ashtabula, Cleveland, Conneaut, and Toledo are busy Lake Erie ports. Barges tie up at Cincinnati on the Ohio River.

Ohio takes in about $9 billion every year from tourism. Restaurants, hotels, state parks, and museums form Ohio's tourist industry.

Chapter 6

Seeing the Sights

Ohio offers many wonderful sights to visitors. The state parks have caves and high waterfalls. Ohio also has the homes of five United States presidents. Many people visit its museums and zoos.

Northwestern Ohio

Several islands lie off Ohio's northwest Lake Erie shore. Inscription Rock is on Kelleys Island. Early Indians carved pictures into this rock.

South Bass Island is to the northwest. Put-in-Bay is a resort village on the island. A tall granite column rises above Put-in-Bay. This is the Perry Victory and International Peace Memorial. The column celebrates Commodore Oliver H. Perry's victory over the English during the War of 1812.

Toledo is on Ohio's mainland. The Toledo Zoo has 400 different animal species. Nearby is Maumee

Waterfalls tumble over the Hocking River in Hocking Hills State Park. It is southeast of Columbus.

Bay State Park. Bird-watchers can see many shore birds there.

Sandusky is east along the lakeshore. It is a great resort city. Battery Park has a swimming pool with waves. Cedar Point's beach draws many swimmers, too. Cedar Point also has an amusement park. Visitors get chills and thrills on its roller coasters.

Milan is south of Sandusky. Thomas A. Edison was born there. The Edison Birthplace Museum is open to visitors.

Northeastern Ohio

Oberlin is east of Milan. Oberlin College is there. This was the nation's first college to admit African Americans and women.

To the east is the Cuyahoga Valley National Recreation Area. This land lies along the Cuyahoga River. Visitors can ride the Cuyahoga Valley Line Railroad. It runs between Cleveland and Akron.

Riders can stop at the Hale Farm and Village. Settlers from Connecticut lived there. Today, guides show visitors how the pioneers cooked.

Akron is the home of Inventure Place. This museum honors America's **inventors**. Visitors can try being inventors there.

Canton is to the south. The Pro Football Hall of Fame is there. It honors football's best players, coaches, and sportswriters.

Central Ohio

Columbus is Ohio's largest city. It is also the state capital. Ohioans call the short, round capitol building the Hatbox. Ohio State University is in Columbus.

Marion is north of Columbus. This was the home of President Warren G. Harding. Harding gave speeches from the front porch. Visitors can tour his home.

The Moundbuilders State Memorial is east of Columbus. Its earth wall circles 26 acres (10 hectares) of land.

Southeastern Ohio

Hocking Hills State Park is southeast of Columbus. High waterfalls tumble over the Hocking River. Caves there have strangely shaped rocks. One is called the Devil's Bathtub.

Marietta is farther southeast. It lies on the Ohio River. This is Ohio's oldest non-Indian settlement. Today, visitors can tour Rossi Pasta. They can see how pasta is made.

Southwestern Ohio

Cincinnati sits in far southwestern Ohio. Visitors there enjoy the Cincinnati Zoo. They come to see rare Komodo dragons. These animals weigh about 300 pounds (135 kilograms).

To the northeast is Dayton. Nearby is the United States Air Force Museum. It displays hundreds of military aircraft.

To the southeast is Ripley. Rankin House overlooks the Ohio River. This was an important stop on the Underground Railroad. John Rankin hid more than 2,000 slaves there.

North of Ripley is Serpent Mound. It is about 5 feet (1.5 meters) high. It is more than 1,000 feet

(300 meters) long. It winds back and forth like a giant snake.

Farther northeast is the Mound City Group National Monument. Visitors can see 23 ancient burial mounds.

Ohio Time Line

10,000 B.C.—The first people arrive in Ohio.

700 B.C.-A.D. 500—Early people build huge mounds in southern Ohio.

1669—Robert Cavelier, Sieur de La Salle, is believed to be the first non-Indian to travel through Ohio.

1750—Christopher Gist of Virginia's Ohio Company explores Ohio.

1787—Ohio becomes part of the Northwest Territory, which is controlled by the United States.

1788—Marietta, Ohio's first non-Indian town, is founded on the Ohio River.

1794—Indians are defeated at the Battle of Fallen Timbers.

1795—In the Greenville Treaty, Ohio's Indians give the United States government two-thirds of Ohio.

1803—Ohio becomes the 17th state.

1813—Commodore Oliver H. Perry wins the Battle of Lake Erie against the British in the War of 1812.

1832—The Ohio and Erie Canal links the Ohio River and Lake Erie.

1837—Oberlin College opens its doors to women, becoming the nation's first coeducational college.

1856—Wilberforce University becomes the nation's first college for African Americans.

1863—Southern cavalry raid Ohio and are captured by Union forces at Salineville.

1869—The Cincinnati Red Stockings become the nation's first professional baseball team.

1870—John D. Rockefeller organizes the Standard Oil Company in Cleveland.

1913—Floods kill more than 400 people and cause $250 million in property damage.

1922—The Miami River Valley flood-control project is completed.

1955—The Ohio Turnpike is opened.

1967—Carl Stokes is elected mayor of Cleveland, becoming the first African-American mayor of a major American city.

1970—Four students are killed at Kent State University by National Guard troops during a Vietnam War protest.

1974—Ohio State University wins the Rose Bowl.

1985—A tornado kills nine people in Niles and destroys much of Newton Falls.

1990—The Cincinnati Reds win the World Series.

1995—The Rock and Roll Hall of Fame and Museum opens in Cleveland; Bosnian peace talks are held at Wright-Patterson Air Force Base.

Famous Ohioans

Neil Armstrong (1930-) Astronaut who became the first person to walk on the moon, on July 20, 1969; born in Wapakoneta.

Daniel Beard (1850-1941) Founder and leader of the Boy Scouts of America; born in Cincinnati.

Thomas A. Edison (1847-1931) Inventor of the phonograph, incandescent light bulb, and hundreds of other products; born in Milan.

Harvey Firestone (1868-1938) Founder of Akron's Firestone Tire and Rubber Company; born in Columbiana.

Ulysses S. Grant (1822-1885) Civil War general who became head of the Union army in 1864; served as 18th president of the United States (1869-1877); born in Point Pleasant.

Margaret Hamilton (1902-1985) Movie actress who played the Wicked Witch of the West in *The Wizard of Oz*; born in Cleveland.

Maya Lin (1959-) Sculptor and architect who designed the Vietnam Veterans Memorial and the Civil Rights Memorial; born in Athens.

Toni Morrison (1931-) Pulitzer Prize-winning author of *Beloved*; born in Lorain.

Jesse Owens (1913-1980) Ohio State University track star who won four gold medals at the 1936 Summer Olympic Games.

Pontiac (1720-1769) Ottawa Indian chief who united Indian tribes in Pontiac's War (1763) against the British; born in northern Ohio.

Pete Rose (1941-) Player for and manager of the Cincinnati Reds; all-time leading hitter in 1986; banned from baseball for gambling; born in Cincinnati.

Steven Spielberg (1947-) Filmmaker who directed *E.T.*, *Jaws*, *Raiders of the Lost Ark*, and other popular movies; born in Cincinnati.

Gloria Steinem (1934-) Writer and leader of the women's rights movement; a founder of *Ms.* magazine; born in Toledo.

Tecumseh (1768-1813) Shawnee chief who tried to unite Indian tribes against white settlers; sided with the British in the War of 1812; born near Piqua.

James Thurber (1894-1961) Cartoonist and humor writer; born in Columbus.

Wilbur Wright (1867-1912) and **Orville Wright** (1871-1948) Brothers who invented the first successful airplane; Wilbur was born in Indiana, and Orville was born in Dayton.

Glossary

ancestor—a person from whom one is descended, such as a grandmother or a great-grandfather

canal—a human-made waterway that connects rivers and lakes

colony—a group of people who settle in a distant land but remain under control of their native country.

deejay—a radio host who makes announcements and plays music

glacier—a huge, slow-moving sheet of ice

humid—air that is heavy with moisture

immigrant—one who comes to another country to settle

inventor—someone who discovers a new or better way of doing something

lyrics—the words of a song

manufacturing—the making of products

missionary—people sent to do religious or charitable work in a territory or foreign country

plateau—large area of land with a flat surface that rises above the surrounding land

pollution—the dirtying of the air, water, or ground

refuge—a place where animals are protected

reservation—land set aside for Native Americans

surrender—to lay down arms or give up during a war

To Learn More

Brown, Dottie. *Ohio*. Hello USA. Minneapolis: Lerner Publications, 1993.

Fradin, Dennis B. *Ohio*. From Sea to Shining Sea. Chicago: Children's Press, 1993.

Kent, Deborah. *Ohio*. America the Beautiful. Chicago: Children's Press, 1994.

Zimmeth, Khristi Sigurdson. *Ohio Family Adventure Guide: Great Things to See and Do for the Entire Family*. Old Saybrook, Conn.: The Globe Pequot Press, 1996.

Internet Sites

City.Net Ohio
http://www.city.net/countries/united_states/ohio
Travel.org-Ohio
http://travel.org/ohio.html
State of Ohio Front Page
http://ohio.gov/
Go Explore Ohio
http://www.go-explore.com/

Useful Addresses

Pro Football Hall of Fame
2121 George Halas Drive Northwest
Canton, OH 44708

Rock and Roll Hall of Fame and Museum
1 Key Plaza
Cleveland, OH 44114

Serpent Mound State Memorial
3850 State Route 73
Peebles, OH 45660

Thomas A. Edison Birthplace Museum
9 Edison Drive
Milan, OH 44846

United States Air Force Museum
Wright-Patterson Air Force Base
Dayton, OH 45433

Index